THE DIABOLO BOOK

THE DIABOLO BOOK

BY TODD STRONG

BRIAN DUBÉ, INC. NEW YORK

Published in the United States by Brian Dubé, Inc.
Manufactured in the United States of America

Library of Congress Cataloging-in-Publication Data

Strong, Todd, 1953-
    The diabolo book / by Todd Strong.
        p.   cm.
    ISBN 0-917643-10-0
    1. Diabolo (Game)   I. Title
GV1216.S77   1994
794- - dc20   93-43737

First Printing, March 1994
Second Printing, November 1996

Cover - Barrett Felker
Cover Photography - Warren Tang
Illustrations - Linda Gilligan-Rivera
Le Leuch & Korthaus Photograph - Verena Blank
Cover Design - Shelley Fisher
Book Design by Kyoko Yabuki

CONTENTS

Acknowledgements

This is the fun part. I'd like to thank all the people who either helped me learn how to play with diabolos or helped with some aspect of this book. I'm sure I have left some people out. To all of you, thanks.

Andrew Allen

Ngaio Bealum

Geoffrey Budworth

Hovey Burgess

Adrienne Burk

Andrea Cornell

Andrew Conway

Dave Finnigan

Zhan Gao

Michael Genahr

Linda Gilligan-Rivera

Pat Gray

Susan Hall

Karen Heil

Andrea Honier

Nikolaus Holz

Mrs. Houchins

Richard Jacquot

Karin Johnson

Larry Kluger

Michael Korthaus

Gilles Le Leuch

Bill Marshak

Jeff Mason

Pierre Morère

Narbo

Robert Nelson

Tom Nesbit

Larry Olson

p

Parker Brothers

Dyak ReVeal

Jo Riley

Andy Robinson

Tom Roos

Allan Rumpf

Jochen Schell

Michael Schubach

Edward Shafer

Shenyang Acrobatic Troupe

Kezia Tenenbaum

Dr. Tenenbaum

Bob Vanderwilt

Kevin Wenzel

Wanda Wenzel

Grant White

Susie Williams

Jeff Wood

Ye Wei

Karl-Heinz Ziethen

Sometimes institutions can be very helpful. These were:

International Jugglers Association
European Jugglers Association
Centre National des Arts du Cirque
Smithsonian
Bethnal Green Museum of Childhood
Pollack's Toy Museum

Aren't libraries great? I had the help and assistance of several to research the history of the diabolo. Particularly helpful were:

Seattle Public Library
San Francisco Public Library
Library of Congress
Royal British Library
Newcastle Public Library
La Bibliotheque National de France
La Bibliotheque Publiqe de Châlons-sur-Marne

The libraries at the following universities were also helpful:

University of Washington
University of Texas, Austin
University of Colorado, Boulder
UC Berkeley
UCLA
McNair Library

This book was originally written as a paper to satisfy part of the graduation requirements for the Master of Science degree in Experiential Education at Mankato State University, Minnesota. Out of acorns...

John Held

Jeff Mason

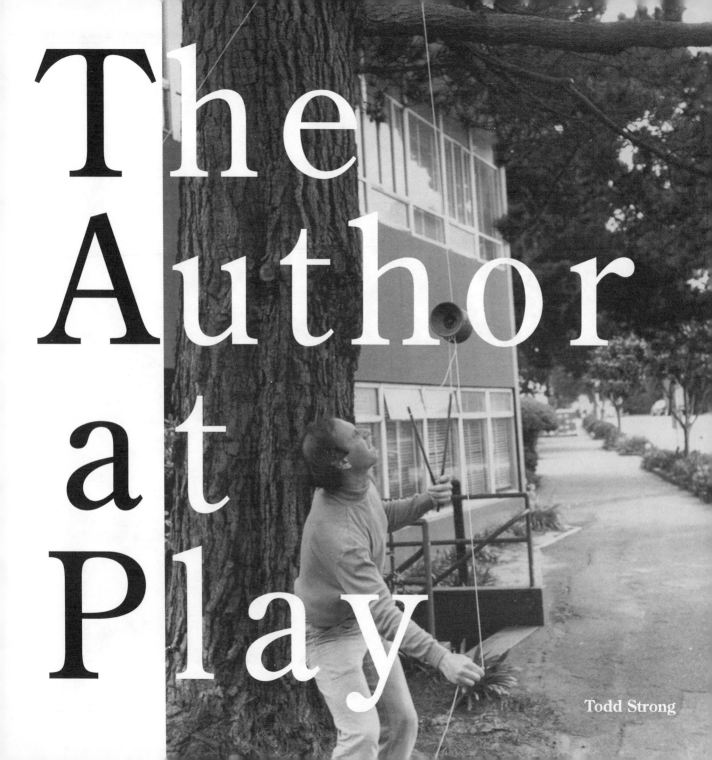

The Author at Play

Todd Strong

Introduction

The diabolo fits into the large family of gyroscopic toys. People throughout the ages have found pleasure and amusement in spinning things. From the tops and yo-yos where you do the spinning to the large Ferris Wheels and merry-go-rounds where you are spun, circular motion seems to hold a universal fascination.

Diabolos and Players of Yesteryear
Real Diabolo by C. B. Fry, London 1907.

Why Play With the Diabolo?

I see several possible benefits that can be derived from learning to spin a diabolo. You may fit into one or more of these categories. Many people will play with the diabolo for the simple fun and amusement it offers as a toy. Think of it as a more active form of solitaire. Lots of folks will take diabolos to parks and play catch with one another much as Frisbee players do now; a great way to spend an afternoon with friends. You can use your skill with the diabolo to impress and entertain others at picnics and social gatherings. Go ahead, show off a little bit. In fact, some people may concentrate on learning a smooth routine and will start to perform professionally with the diabolo. Your new hobby may make you a little extra money.

For those of you who have never heard of a diabolo before, let me tell you what it does. The idea with this toy is to use the string connecting the handsticks to spin and manipulate the diabolo. This is done by passing the string under the axle of the diabolo and causing it to rotate.

Oh, by the way, spinning a diabolo is considered a type of juggling. It is one of the few juggling skills that is non-symmetrical. That is, there is a definite right or left hand dominance with this sport. Since the majority of people using the diabolo will begin with a right hand drive (even though I am left-handed, I first learned how to spin a diabolo right-handed), this book is written right-handed. To learn the tricks left-handed, switch everything.

(You lefties are used to this!)

Lots of 'up', 'down', 'right', and 'left' directions are used. Some of the tricks will only work out one way. Others are presented in a particular fashion because most people find it easier to learn in that direction. By all means, please experiment. If another approach feels better, try it. Think of these pages as suggestions. Should you know of or devise a new variation, I would love to hear about it.

Pete Seeger compares a song book to a photograph of a bird in flight. The picture may be pretty, but it can only hint at the beauty of the live bird actually flying. Just so, he advises, one must sing the songs in the book in order to make them come alive. Think of this volume as a song book for the diabolo. The magic comes when you use the ideas to get the diabolo flying.

Perhaps you are the type who likes to challenge yourself and explore your hidden potentials. Any time you stumble onto a new set of skills or tricks to master, you consider it a rare treat. You can use the diabolo to open up acres of unexplored territory. While exploring all the possibilities of this toy don't forget about your own personal self-exploration. "How do I best learn things, from a book or from other people? When do I get frustrated and what do I do when I am frustrated?" Learning the diabolo or any other new skill lets you rediscover your strengths and weaknesses. Watch your reactions to success and failure when trying new tricks. Finally, to carry this full circle, you can share your knowledge with others. How does the pupil become the teacher? What is the clearest way to pass on the excitement and fun of this toy to others?

Congratulations on buying this book and thank you for your interest in diabolos. I became fascinated with the diabolo about ten years ago and have been spinning one ever since. I trust you, too, will soon fall under the spell.

Fred Garbo

Fred Garbo

1· Getting Started

Let's set up some common terms and directions to establish a shared vocabulary. A diabolo set consists of two handsticks attached by a string, and a diabolo, that two-wheeled thing connected by an axle (fig. 1).

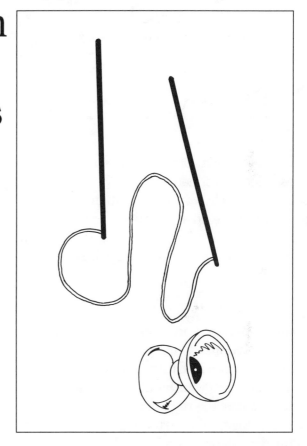

Fig. 1. Diabolo With Handsticks

The string should be as long as the distance between your chin and your toes. Of course, you can use a shorter or longer string if you like. My advice is to go shorter rather than longer for added control. I use this chin-to-toe length for one diabolo and switch to a shorter string when I spin two diabolos. That's for later.

Personal preferences run hot and heavy on what is the best type of string to use. I use a thin nylon braided string that gets replaced when it's dirty or frayed, and it seems to work just fine. A kite store is a good place to find string.

Diabolo Terms

A traditional Chinese diabolo has two wheels instead of hemispheres. Sound holes are cut into the hollow wheels so when the diabolo is spinning, the holes whistle.

Stand with a handstick in each hand and rest the diabolo on the center of the string in front of you.

If we split your body vertically in half there is a right and a left side. Your right hand is holding the right handstick. Imagine two vertical planes running through your arms and divide the space into three zones. The inside zone is between your hands while there are two outside zones, the right and the left.

A horizontal line running through the axle of the diabolo creates a top and a bottom half.

Finally, imagine you are standing right up to a wall so both of your handsticks would actually touch the wall. This is the 'wall plane.' You carry an imaginary wall plane with you, perpendicular to your line of sight and running through the ends of your handsticks. Most of the diabolo tricks are done in this wall plane.

Home position is right here in this illustration (fig. 2). The diabolo is in front of you, a little bit lower than your waist.

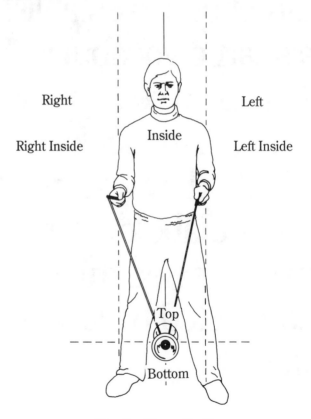

Fig. 2. Home Position

Two Methods to Start Spinning the Diabolo

Ready? I'm going to explain several different ways to start spinning your diabolo. Each one works fine and they don't contradict each other. Try them all to see which ones you prefer. If you have a favorite, that's great. Using the other methods also helps you to understand the feel of a diabolo.

Starting the Diabolo in the Air

Place the diabolo on the string and jerk your right hand quickly up and down (fig. 3). Go for very small, quick movements. Your left hand doesn't move at all. Before you know it, the diabolo should begin turning counterclockwise as you are looking at it. Keep up the small, fast jerks with just the right hand.

When your right hand jerks the string up it spins the diabolo counterclockwise and also raises it a bit higher. The diabolo falls as you quickly lower your right hand. When the diabolo has fallen on the string making the string

taut you are ready to jerk your hand up again for another cycle to add more spin.

This is an excellent way for a complete beginner to learn to spin a diabolo. By concentrating on using only the right hand you will not be confused about how to coordinate your arms along with the diabolo. Also, while you might not have the exact rhythm right away, by making extremely small, quick jerks, the diabolo starts spinning. Once you can spin a diabolo you will want to change to other techniques to get more speed.

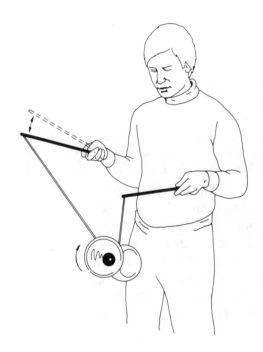

Fig. 3. Spinning the Diabolo

Starting the Diabolo From the Ground

Start with your handsticks pointed down in front of you so the string is stretched out on the ground in the wall plane. The diabolo should straddle the string, close to the tip of the right handstick (fig. 4).

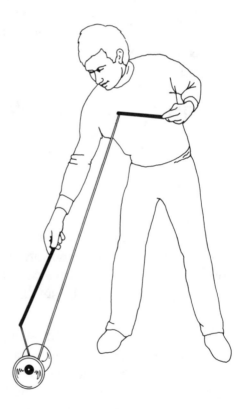

IMPORTANT FACT!

⊗ The diabolo only spins in one direction. This can either be clockwise (left-handed) or counterclockwise (right-handed). Even though I am left-handed I spin the diabolo right-handed. The advice given in this book is for a right-handed spin. You lefties are used to switching things around if you want to spin left-handed.

Fig. 4. Second Way to Spin Diabolo

Raise your right hand and handstick straight up so the string to the right of the diabolo rolls the diabolo over towards the other side (fig. 5). As the diabolo nears the left handstick raise both hands to lift both the string and the diabolo off the ground.

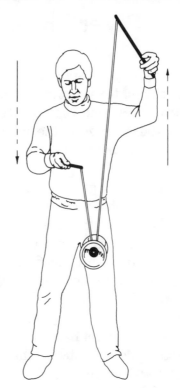

Fig. 6. Recovery Stroke

Recovery Stroke

Now you must quickly reposition the string so the diabolo is near the right handstick again. This is called the recovery stroke.

For the recovery stroke quickly slide the string under the axle of the diabolo so the diabolo ends up back near the right handstick (fig. 6). If you lower your right hand faster than you raise your left hand the string slides under the axle and does not slow down the spin.

Fig. 5. Beginning From the Ground

Power Stroke

The power stroke spins the diabolo while bringing it closer to the left handstick. For the power stroke raise your right hand slowly enough so the string grabs the axle of the diabolo and spins it counterclockwise (fig. 7).

The motion is a grab-slip, grab-slip. The grab is the power stroke and the slip is the recovery stroke. For a right hand drive raise your right hand slowly enough so the string grabs the diabolo, causing it to spin. Think of a fan belt turning a pulley. For the recovery stroke lower your right hand so fast the string doesn't catch on the axle and slow down the diabolo. The grab of the power stroke lasts longer than the slip of the recovery stroke. The timing is actually graaaab-slip, graaaaab-slip.

Concentrate on your right hand. Use your wrist to almost jerk the string up and down. Your left hand should keep pretty still for this as in the first technique. Notice that the power stroke raises the diabolo up a few inches as well as spins it counterclockwise. During the recovery stroke the diabolo is falling with the string so the string can't bind on the axle to slow the spin.

Some Thoughts

The motion of the diabolo is gyroscopic. Once it is spinning it becomes very stable. The hardest part in learning to use your diabolo is to start from a stationary position and get it spinning. Maintaining an already spinning diabolo is actually much easier than starting one from scratch.

If possible have a friend who can already use a diabolo begin the spin and hand you the handsticks when the diabolo is stable. Once you get the feel of maintaining the spin you will find it easier to begin on your own.

You can get good feedback on how well you are doing by noticing if the diabolo is spinning smoothly or if it has a wobble. Good form is nice and smooth.

Additionally, the authentic Chinese diabolos are built with sound holes that will whistle if the diabolo is spun quickly and properly. You can hear as well as see a good diaboloist.

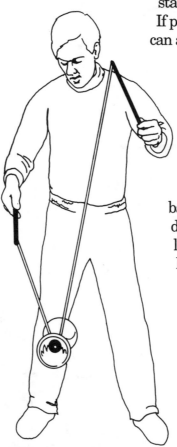

Fig. 7. Power Stroke

Variations on Loops of String Around the Axle

Some people prefer to loop the string completely around the axle of the diabolo rather than just a half-loop with the diabolo straddling the string (fig. 8). You get a lot more control but run the risk of having the string tangle up on itself and racing up towards the left handstick out of control. You'll see what I mean after this happens. To avoid this runaway diabolo, place your left hand slightly in front of the wall plane and your right hand slightly behind the wall plane so the string doesn't bind on itself. In addition, pay close attention to the tension on the string. You don't want it to get too tight.

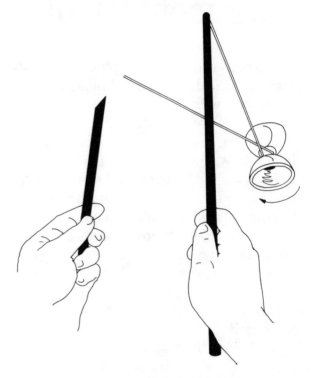

Fig. 9. Half-Loop Twist

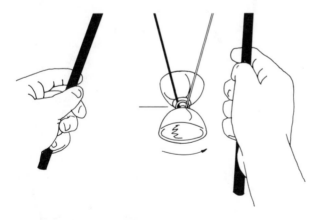

Fig. 8. Full Loop of String Around Axle

Others like to use a half-loop but then twist the string once for a bit more control (fig. 9). The diabolo will then spin clockwise instead of counterclockwise as you look at it. Try all the variations and see which works best for you.

Smooth It Out

As you get comfortable spinning the diabolo start to smooth out your technique. Instead of jerking your wrist up and down, start from the shoulder and use your whole arm. Coordinate your left arm so it moves up and down in opposition with your right. Again, on the power stroke as the right hand rises, lower your left hand slowly enough to keep enough tension on the string to spin the diabolo counterclockwise. On the recovery stroke lower your right hand quickly as you raise your left so the string glides under the axle without slowing down the spin.

A good, fast spin is the result of long, quick strokes. The faster you complete each cycle, the faster the diabolo spins and the more stable it becomes. Also, the longer the stroke, or the more string you use, the faster the diabolo spins. Combining these two techniques, speed and length, gives you the best results. Remember, long, quick, and smooth strokes.

Correcting Tilts and Twists

Two problems may arise while you are spinning the diabolo. Both are described below with the appropriate corrective measures.

The Tilting Diabolo

The first is when the diabolo tips out of a horizontal plane; that is the front wheel becomes higher or lower than the rear wheel (fig. 10).

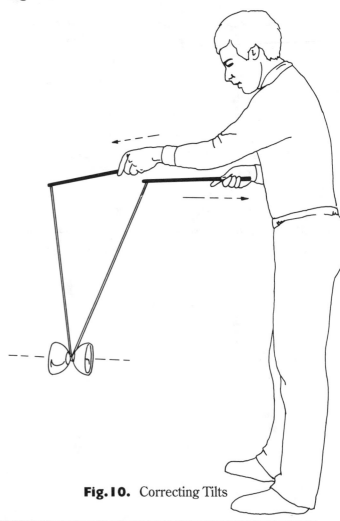

Fig. 10. Correcting Tilts

Correct this tilt by adjusting your drive hand (right hand) horizontally. Extending your right hand forward past the wall plane lowers the front wheel and raises the back wheel. Pulling your right hand behind the wall plane raises the front wheel and lowers the back wheel.

Another way to think about this is to watch how the string moves under the axle. If both your hands are in the wall plane, the string is at a ninety degree angle to the axle of the diabolo. If your right hand is in front of or behind the wall plane, the string is going diagonally across the axle.

I think what affects the tilt is the string on the left hand side of the axle. If the string on the left half of the diabolo is dragging diagonally across the axle, it will pull that wheel up. If you move the left half of the string back then the back wheel comes up.

Of course, it could be that it is the string on the right side of the axle. When I pet a cat it rubs itself into my hand not away from it.

Maybe this is what is happening. Confused? Ask a physicist. Fortunately, it is my hands that need to know this, not my head. Play with moving your hands back and forth as you keep spinning the diabolo and you will see what I mean.

The Twisting Diabolo

The second problem occurs when the diabolo starts to turn away from you out of the wall plane. Don't take it personally, this is normal with gyroscopes. If this happens a lot it may indicate your diabolo is slightly out of balance.

Even though your diabolo may be balanced there are still times when it turns away from you. If you are doing a show and want to swing the diabolo back around to face the audience there are some techniques that allow you to make the turn without having to stop and begin from scratch.

You can use your right handstick to brush the diabolo around. If you brush the tip of your right handstick against the rear wheel, the diabolo will turn counterclockwise (fig. 11). If you bring your right hand in front of the wall plane and push the front wheel, the diabolo will turn clockwise (fig. 12). I find it easiest to turn my wrist around backward when I make this front wheel correction.

Fig. 11. Counterclockwise Corrrection of Diabolo

Fig. 12. Clockwise Correction of Diabolo

Warning!

Be careful about applying too much pressure; there is a tendency for the diabolo to tip out of the horizontal plane with this move. Should this happen just bring your right hand forward or back (whichever is appropriate) to correct it back to horizontal. Once you have adjusted your position you are ready to get on with the show.

This correction is fairly sophisticated. Don't feel you must master it before going on the learn other tricks. Just realize that you must always face the rear wheel and you need to walk around in order to keep the proper orientation if your diabolo turns. Think of it as a dance with your diabolo leading you about the dance floor and it may not be as frustrating.

If you want to learn two diabolos you should not turn your wrist around to correct the front wheel. Just get used to tapping it lightly with the tip of the handstick and don't make any strange changes with your wrist. You don't have time to turn your wrist around with two diabolos.

The Diabolo Out of Balance

✪ Sometimes diabolos get out of balance. An unbalanced diabolo's axis tends to slowly rotate in a circle as you spin it. This is called precession. It's important to recognize the problem and know how to correct it.

While some of us will tolerate walking around in a circle following the diabolo's slow rotation, the professional diabolist finds it awkward to do a show with his or her back turned to the audience for a good deal of the performance. Perhaps this is why theater in the round was developed.

It is a simple matter to put your diabolo back into balance. If your diabolo tends to pull you around counterclockwise as you look down on it, your rear wheel is heavier than your front wheel. You need to add some weight to the front wheel. If the diabolo pulls you around clockwise then the front wheel is heavier and weight should be added to the rear wheel.

I use ordinary washers to add weight to the appropriate wheel. Unscrew the nut, add a washer and you should have it. Sometimes it takes a combination of two or more washers to get the balance right, just keep playing with it until your diabolo is steady.

Jochen Schell

2·Teaching Your Diabolo Some Tricks

Now that your have learned the basic techniques of spin-ning and controlling the diabolo, you are ready for some tricks !

Postcard, England 1908

Introduction to the Advanced Moves

This chapter is the heart of the book. Learning all these tricks will take some time and effort but, in a way, that is the fun part. You can look forward to hours of challenge and excitement. If everyone could perform all these tricks perfectly the first time, there would be no challenge and the diabolo would get boring. Initial failure coupled with consistent improvement on all the variations has spurred me on to new patterns I could not have imagined just a few years back. Even now I spend more time working on the tricks I can't do rather than the tricks I can do. An appropriate attitude might be: dropping is learning.

These variations are presented in the approximate order that most people will learn them. Learning the tricks at the beginning of the chapter develops the skills you will need when attempting the harder tricks later on. For example, it would be very difficult to learn how to spin two diabolos without first being able to do *Hop Overs* well.

Begin at the beginning, but don't wait to perfect each trick before going on to the next. Working on several different tricks and skills at the same time will broaden your understanding of the diabolo. The familiarity gained through working on different tricks will have a cumulative effect and make you a better player.

There is a difference between depth and breadth in learning. Depth is how well you can perform one trick. Breadth is how many different styles and variations you can do. You should try to improve both your depth and your breadth at the same time. Strategies and clues about working with the diabolo are scattered throughout these pages. Working on one technique will help with the others.

Challenge yourself to improve each time you practice and the sessions will stay fresh and exciting.

I find the best way to approach learning the diabolo is with an easy, relaxed, fun attitude. Picking up the diabolo briefly several times during the day is more rewarding than one extended session.

You may want to practice to music. I am pretty conscientious about my practice and try to put in at least forty-five minutes a day. By turning on a cassette tape recorder, not only is there music in the background but I have a built in clock, as well. If the practice session is interrupted, I turn the tape off. Right before the practice is resumed I start the music again. When the tape is over I know that a good forty-five minute workout has occurred without having to watch the clock.

Throws and Catches

Hey there, hot shot! You can start and keep a pretty good spin going and now you want to get fancy. One of the more exciting aspects of the diabolo is that you can play catch with it, either alone or with a partner.

To throw a diabolo just snap your arms open and toss upward. Spread your hands quickly out to each side and flick your wrists up (fig. 13). The harder you throw your arms open and the quicker you flick your wrists up, the higher the diabolo soars. That's how

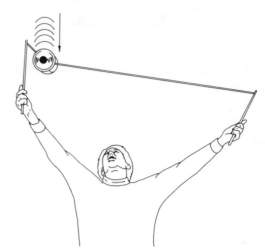

Fig. 14. Catching the Diabolo

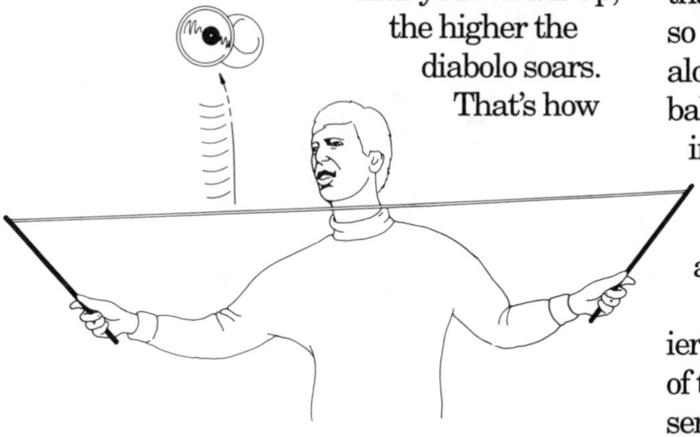

Fig.13. Throwing the Diabolo Upward

you throw a diabolo. Even more important now is how to catch one; especially if you are trying out each move as you read this.

To catch a diabolo keep the string taut and raise your right hand in front of you higher than your head. Point your right handstick out so it extends the line of your arm and sight along it as you would a tennis racket or a base-ball glove. Catch the diabolo on the string just inside the tip of the right handstick (fig. 14).

When the diabolo is on the string, cushion the fall by quickly lowering your right hand and raising your left.

Catching near the handstick is much easier than trying to catch a diabolo in the middle of the string. If you think about it, this makes sense. All of our lives we have been catching things either in our hands or in something that was an extension of our hands. There are few items we catch three feet to the left of our right hand. Now you can use all that catching practice to snag the diabolo from its imminent appointment with the ground.

Jump Rope

How many times can you jump over the string while the diabolo is in the air? Here are some strategy hints to help you: 1) toss the diabolo high and accurately, you don't want to have to run to another spot to make the catch; 2) jump the string quickly; and 3) don't forget to catch it (fig. 15).

Behind the Back Catch

Instead of placing your right hand overhead and in front of you, put it behind you (fig. 16). After you make the catch, pivot one full turn to your right and you will be back in home position with an untangled string.

Fig. 15. Jumping Rope

Fig. 16. Behind the Back Catch

Catch on the Handstick

Turn your wrist 90 degrees so the handstick is in the wall plane and catch the diabolo on the handstick rather than the string. Caution: A spinning diabolo tends to roll along the handstick. To keep it steady tilt the handstick a little. Tilt your right hand up and your left hand down to counter-act the spin (fig.17). The diabolo may also turn out of the wall plane. Move the handstick diagonally back and forth to guide the diabolo back into the wall plane.

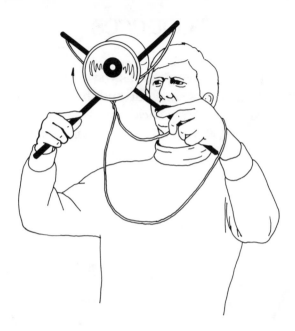

Fig. 18. Catch on Crossed Handsticks

Catch on Crossed Handsticks

Cross your handsticks in front of you and catch the diabolo at the intersection of the X made by the handsticks (fig. 18). (Hint, this is much easier if the handsticks are at a shallow angle, less than forty-five degrees.) Flick the diabolo back up, make the string taught overhead and catch it again on the string to continue spinning.

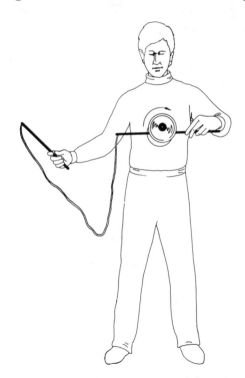

Fig. 17. Catch on the Handstick

Bounces

Keep the string taut as you catch the diabolo. Immediately push up and the diabolo will bounce off the string back into the air. With practice you can get off several bounces in a row (fig. 19).

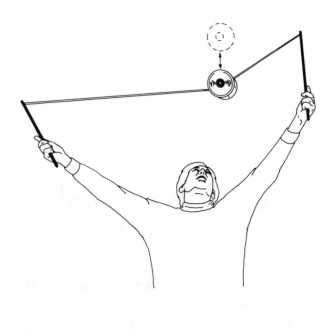

Fig. 19. Bounces

Continuous Throws

You can actually add spin to the diabolo while you are throwing it. When you hold your right hand higher than your left and catch the diabolo near the tip of the right handstick you create a ramp of string down which the diabolo can roll. The diabolo now rolls down the string adding spin. (If you switch so your left hand is higher, the ramp of string goes the wrong way and the diabolo slows down.) When the diabolo has rolled over to the left handstick you again throw it into the air. Lead a bit with your right hand as you throw to also add some last second spin (fig. 20).

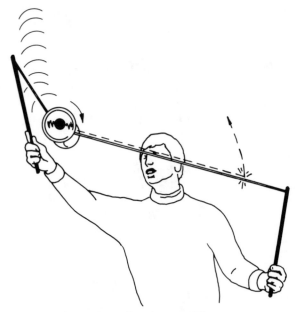

Fig. 20. Continuous Throws

Roll Alongs

Tie a long length of string between two trees or signs about 2-3 feet off the ground. Once the diabolo is spinning set it down on the horizontal string and watch it take off for the other side. If you hurry you should be able to keep pace with the traveling diabolo and pick it up again (fig. 21A).

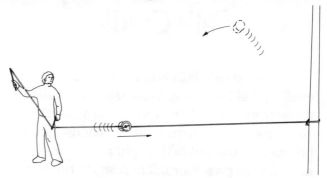

Fig. 21B. Snap Backs

String Around the Neck

After you throw the diabolo place the string around your neck and turn sideways so you are in the wall plane. You now have a choice of two sections of string on which to catch the diabolo (fig. 22).

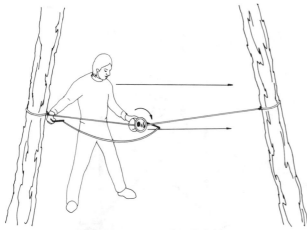

Fig. 21A. Roll Alongs

Snap Backs

Tie some string around a tree at about waist height and secure the other end to your left handstick. Let the diabolo roll along off your string onto the string tied to the tree. When the diabolo gets about three-quarters of the way to the tree snap it back with a sharp pull from your left hand (fig. 21B).

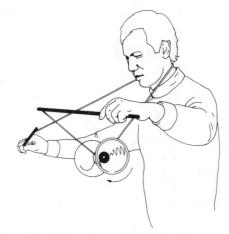

Fig. 22. String Around the Neck

Cat's Cradle

While the diabolo is in the air make a cat's cradle out of the string. Make the cat's cradle by passing your right handstick underneath the string coming down from the left handstick and bringing it back out to the right about three inches. Now pass your left handstick through the large loop in the string and bring it back out to the left. Spread your hands apart and the string should look like an underlined letter 'x'.

Hold the handsticks vertically and catch the diabolo at the intersection of the X (fig.23).

Or point the handsticks in towards you and catch the diabolo on the underline (fig. 24). Toss it up, point your handsticks down at the ground with the tips angled in towards each other and spread your arms to untangle the string. Reach up and catch the diabolo on the untangled string.

Fig. 23. Cat's Cradle

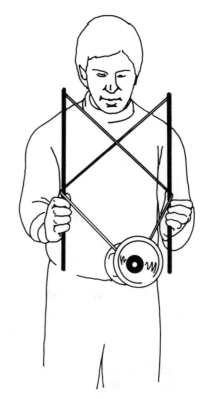

Fig. 24. Diabolo Caught on Underline

Cat's Cradle Variation #1

An easier way to get into a cat's cradle is to swap the handsticks. Pass your right handstick over the left and change handsticks (fig. 25, 26).

Now you have a cat's cradle without the string wrapped around the axle of the diabolo (fig. 27). You can toss the diabolo straight up without it having to climb the string.

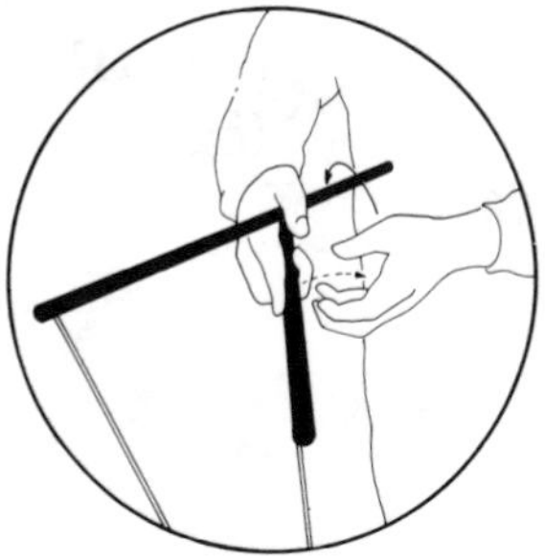

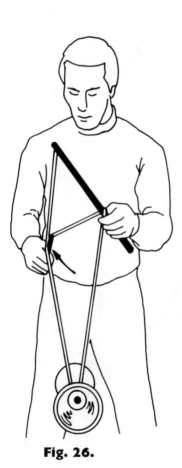

Fig. 25. Switch Handsticks and Eliminate the Loop

Fig. 26.

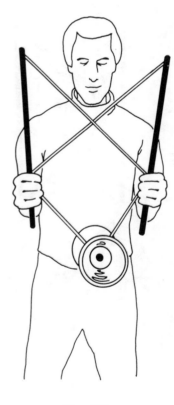

Fig. 27.

Double Cat's Cradle

Go back to the first cat's cradle and this time hook the string with each index finger. You now have a double string cross with the diabolo sitting on the bottom section of string without a loop (fig. 28).You can toss it up and choose either of the two cross points to make the catch.

Fig. 28. Double Cat's Cradle

Pirouettes

Of course, pirouettes while the diabolo is in the air are always a crowd pleaser. If you can do a snappy pirouette without getting dizzy this will even be easier than jumping over the string. (Hmm, I wonder if anyone can play Jump Rope and Pirouette at the same time?) (fig. 29).

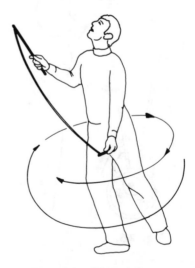

Fig. 29. Pirouettes

Around the Back

Once a diabolo is spinning it's very stable. That's what makes this next trick so easy. Don't tell — people will be impressed if they don't know.

Place your right handstick into your left hand so your left hand is holding both handsticks in a V-shape. Bring your left hand around behind you; when directly behind your back pass the handsticks over to your right hand. The right hand now continues the circle out to the front. Done quickly enough the diabolo will lose very little spin and will still be quite stable after this little stunt (fig. 30).

Around the Head

This is for the brave at heart and the moderately daring. Get a good spin going, raise your arms, and have the diabolo circle your head (fig. 31).

I first learned this carefully by standing in front of a mirror so I could follow the diabolo at all times. I also started with very wide circles and gradually brought them in closer to my head. Wearing a helmet might not be a bad idea.

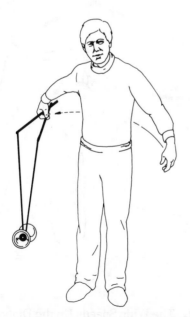

Fig. 30. Around the Back

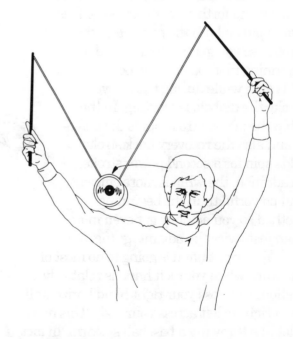

Fig. 31. Around the Head

The Whip

The whip is a great move. Not only is it visually exciting but you can spin the diabolo much more quickly and forcefully than with the beginning method, making the diabolo hum. The faster speed you get from the whip makes it a good technique for those tricks that require a lot of momentum. It is presented a little bit early in this chapter because some of the other moves refer to it. Don't feel you need to master the whip before you go on and try other tricks, though.

To whip the diabolo your right hand crosses back and forth across your body. This provides spin on both the power and the recovery strokes so you get twice the speed. In the beginning method only the power stroke adds spin while during the recovery stroke the diabolo is coasting. In the whip the power stroke spins the diabolo and also the recovery back stroke adds spin for a second power stroke. In addition, the whip is more efficient and powerful than the beginning method so you actually get even more than just twice the advantage (fig. 32).

Your right hand is going to do most of the work while your left hand is relatively stationary. Cross your right hand horizontally from right to left across your body. This move is a lot like throwing a baseball sidearm. In fact, if you want you can even step into the throw with your left leg. The move starts in the shoulder, is carried through the elbow, and finishes with a nice, smooth snapping of your wrist. A key point is to not break your wrist until the end of the stroke. This means the right handstick is pointing back towards the right all the way until you break your wrist at the end.

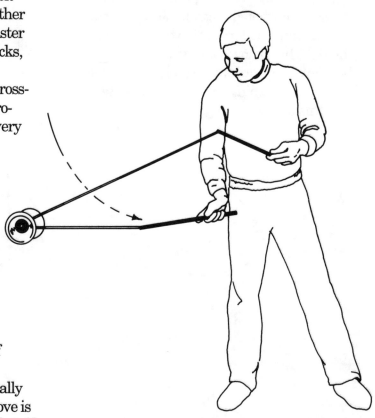

Fig. 32. The Whip Speeds Up the Diabolo

For the back stroke briskly bring your right hand back to its starting position (fig.33). You can feel the string spin the diabolo from underneath the axle during the back stroke. Here you lead with your shoulder, elbow, and then wrist. The handstick trails along to the left of all the action until the end. The diabolo hops from side to side as you whip it.

Hold the handsticks so the string is in the same wall plane of the moving diabolo. The diabolo will hop out of the cradle of the string if the string is out of position. It may take a little practice to see where the diabolo is headed and to adjust your hands so the string is in line, but keep at it.

Remember how you learned to catch the diabolo on the string after throwing it? It's the same idea here only a little more difficult because the string is off to the side instead of overhead, the string is slack instead of taut, and it is moving rather than still.

The same progression applies to the whip as in the beginning technique. As you practice work on getting faster and smoother.

There is a strong tendency for the front wheel of the diabolo to tilt up while doing the whip. To counteract this tilt we use the same principle of moving the right hand in front or back of the wall plane. Corrections are made during the fore stroke by moving your right hand diagonally either forward or back as you sweep across your body.

If the diabolo is tilting up extend your right hand out well in front of you as you stroke across. Keep stroking diagonally in front of you until the diabolo levels out. I find the most effective corrections come from a strong wrist motion. Your right hand can pass either underneath your left hand as you stroke or it can pass above when you make a correction diagonally in front of you. Some people alternate the right hand going over the left one time and then under the left the next. If the diabolo begins to tilt down, stroke your right hand to finish behind the wall plane.

It is normal for the diabolo to tip either one direction or the other.

Alternating between a forward and a backward sweep keeps the diabolo pretty even. If it tilts too far one way, just repeat the appropriate stroke several times in a row to level it out.

Fig. 33. Right Hand Pulls Back with Equal Speed and Force

Climbs

Once you have the diabolo spinning and humming you can make some nice climbs. These tricks really bring out the yo-yo aspect of the diabolo. Remember to start with a good, fast spin.

Use your right hand and handstick to wrap the string around the axle of the diabolo, making one complete loop. Your right hand should end up directly below your left with the string making a straight, vertical line. The diabolo will be suspended in the loop of string just above the right handstick.

Press your right hand down gently and the diabolo will climb up the string. Amazing! Here is what is happening. By pressing down with your right hand you are making a tighter loop and increasing the friction between the spinning axle of the diabolo and the string. The diabolo now has enough grip to actually climb up the string. Notice that the diabolo stays in the loop and the loop moves up and down (fig. 34).

If you press down too hard you can choke the spin of the diabolo and it will slow down to a stop. If you don't press down hard enough there won't be enough friction to make the diabolo climb. As always, you want to follow the Golden Rule and find the middle between two extremes.

Start with a fast spin and by changing the tension of the string you can make the diabolo climb, stop, fall back, and then climb up again. Eventually the diabolo slows down so that you must unwrap the loop and resume spinning.

You can actually have the diabolo climb up and over the left handstick and back down the other side. The string will become twisted and you must either walk around one full turn to untangle it or exchange the handsticks twice.

Extend your right hand in front of the wall plane past the tip of the left handstick and turn your wrist back towards you. Now the loop of string is over the front of the axle rather than the rear.

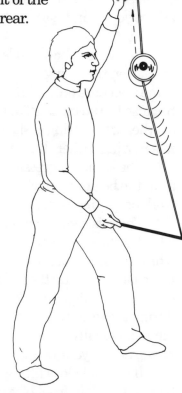

Fig. 34. Climbs

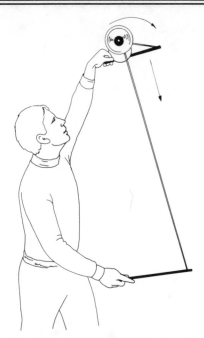

Fig. 35. Diabolo Climbs Over Left Handstick

The diabolo can now clear the top of the left handstick without twisting the string. I find it helps to dip my left handstick down just as the diabolo approaches so it can clear more easily (fig. 35).

High Climbs

Find a nice, tall tree branch and throw some string over it. I'm talking about at least twenty feet here. Anchor one end of the string and leave the other end free. The idea is to transfer the diabolo from your handstick string to the high string and have it climb up to the top.

First get the diabolo screaming. I mean howling. When you get the right speed, place your right handstick into your left hand so your left hand is holding both handsticks in a V-shape.

Hold the diabolo next to the high string with your left hand and with your right hand grab the high string and make a loop around the axle in front of the handstick string. Gently pull the high string down with your right hand, tighten the loop and the diabolo will climb up past the handsticks (fig. 36).

How high you climb depends on how fast a spin you begin with, how quickly you get set up to make the transfer, and how deftly you can control the tension on the high string.

Fig. 36. Diabolo Climbs String

Cat's Cradle Climb

You know, this trick alone is worth the price of this book. By the way, the Chinese call this "climbing the cucumber trellis."

While the diabolo is spinning make a cat's cradle as explained in the throws and catches section. Notice there is now a full loop around the axle and the diabolo is on the underline part of the string (fig. 37).

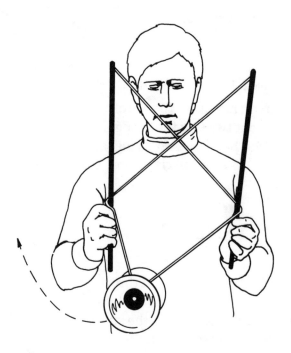

Fig. 37. Combine a String Climb With a Cat's Cradle

Send the diabolo to the right so it passes in front of the right handstick and then back to the left so it is now climbing up the back diagonal section of the string. The diabolo then passes outside the left handstick where it loses the loop (fig. 38). Make both handsticks vertical and catch the diabolo on the cross of the string (fig.39).

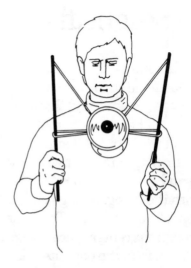

Fig. 39. Catch Diabolo on the Cross of the String

Fig. 38. Around Both Handsticks and Up

Let's break that down to make it easier. Have a friend hold the diabolo stationary on the string while you make a cat's cradle and walk through the sequence a few times.

The diabolo climbs around the cradle from both the friction of the loop as in the string climb and I also move my arms to help it along. This way the loop doesn't have to be as tight and I have less of a chance of losing control. The arm motion is a left, right, left which sends the diabolo to the right, left, right in relation to the handsticks.

String Tricks
Spaghetti

Here's a fun, simple trick to learn. It involves wrapping the string from the right handstick up, over, around, and through the diabolo and the left handstick to make quite a mess. How it all works out still amazes me.

Start by turning your right wrist back in towards you and go over the top of the left handstick with the string. Now go under the axle of the diabolo and back up. This time cut a diagonal through the center space and go over the left handstick from the opposite side. Go straight down and back under the axle of the diabolo (fig.40).

To get out of this just point your handsticks straight down. The weight of the diabolo pulls all the loops of string off the ends of the handsticks. The only problem with this is to do everything fast enough so the diabolo doesn't slow down before you are ready. Ask a friend to hold a non-spinning diabolo a few times so you can get used to the different twists and turns.

Spaghetti Up

If you wrap the string around the diabolo and left handstick one more time and place both handsticks in your left hand you can now toss the diabolo skyward. Make sure you are throwing the diabolo up to the right of both handsticks and not in between them so the string gets untangled (fig. 41).

Fig. 41. Spaghetti Up

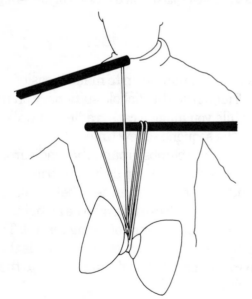

Fig. 40. Spaghetti

Winding the String

The Chinese call this *Winding the String*. So much for their imagination. It's still a great trick, though.

1. Hold the left handstick in the wall plane and pass the right handstick over the left handstick going from the front to the back. Both hands should now be to the left of the diabolo.

2. Pass the string under the axle of the diabolo going from the left to the right.

3. Carry the string up over the handstick from the back to the front while keeping the string to the right of the diabolo. I call this a 'diagonal over' and it seems to help me remember.

4. Go back under the axle from the right to the left and make another 'diagonal over' with the handstick from left to right.

5. Again go under the axle from right to left and then go straight over the handstick to the front, not 'diagonal over.'

6. With your right wrist turned backward pass under the front axle of the diabolo from left to right.

7. Put both handsticks in your left hand with the diabolo between the handsticks. Use your right hand to pull the diabolo out of the string (fig. 42).

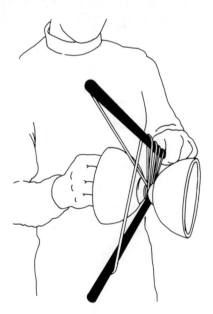

Fig. 42. Pull the Diabolo Out From Between the Handsticks

Around the World

Here we go stealing tricks from yo-yos again.

Swing your arms out and up and the diabolo will describe a large circle trapped in the string (fig. 43). Of course you end up with the string twisted after this but you can either swing back the other way, turn around, or swap the handsticks twice to get untangled.

If you follow the motion with a pirouette the string does not get tangled (fig. 44).

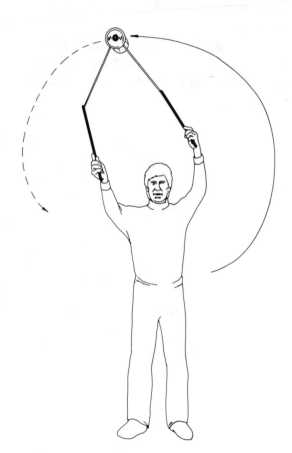

Fig. 43. Around the World

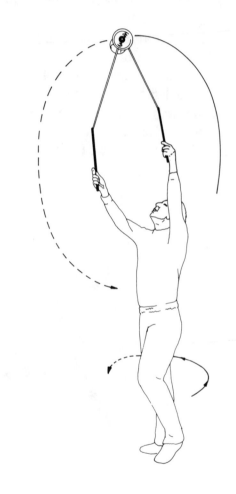

Fig. 44. Pirouette to Keep the String Untangled

Half-way Around the World

If you swing the diabolo up in a smaller circle over the right handstick and let it fall into the center zone between the two handsticks you have just gone half-way around the world (fig.45).

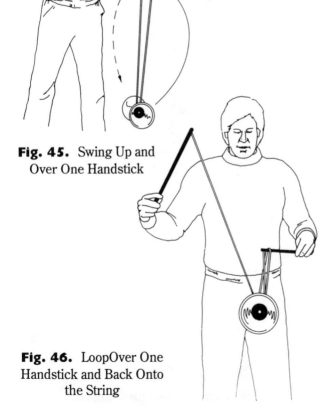

Fig. 45. Swing Up and Over One Handstick

Fig. 46. LoopOver One Handstick and Back Onto the String

Now, rather than just looping the diabolo over the right handstick to hang in space, catch it on the length of string in the center zone. The axle of the diabolo is now supported by two segments of string (fig.46).

By swinging out and over the left handstick you can again catch the diabolo on the string segment in the center zone. This makes an astounding five loops of string under the axle of the diabolo (fig.47).

Of course to get out of these moves just swing back over the left and then back out over the right. Voila, one simple, free-spinning diabolo that has just done some hard traveling.

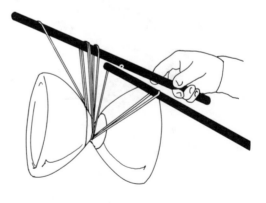

Fig. 47. Swing Over One Handstick and Then the Other

Around the World the Scary Way

After becoming a world traveler and assuring yourself that the diabolo will not fly out of the string you can try some 'guts' around the world.

First check to make sure that your arms are long enough and the string is short enough. Your arms should be slightly longer than one half the length of the string. Make a quarter turn to the right so you face the axle of the diabolo. As you go around the world the diabolo spins out away from you and then heads in towards you. Be careful and remember to have a full arm extension so the diabolo can't smack you upside the head (fig . 48).

Around the Diabolo

If you leave the diabolo stationary and quickly move your arms as if they are pedaling a bicycle you can do repeated around the worlds (fig. 49).

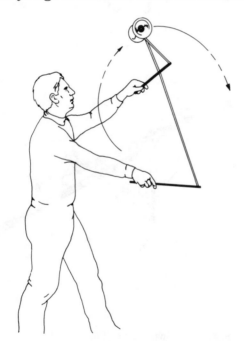

Fig. 48. Around the World the Scary Way

Fig. 49. Around the Diabolo

Hop Overs

Hop Overs are tiny throws of the diabolo over other objects such as your foot or thigh. The diabolo leaves the string, hops over your foot, and is caught on the other side of the string.

For example, place your right foot on the string to the right of the diabolo. Simultaneously step down on the string with your right foot and pull up with your left hand (fig. 50). The diabolo will hop off the string, fly over your foot, and land on the other half of the string. Along with the proper timing you must also match the strength between your foot pressing down and your hand pulling up. The two halves of the string should be in the same plane as the path of the diabolo. If your left hand holds the string too far forward or back the diabolo will hop over your foot all right, but it may land on the cat instead of landing back on the string. You can go the opposite direction but my advice is stick with this and have the diabolo hop over in a clockwise rotation. That way when it rolls down the string on the right side it picks up spin.

Once I learned how to do this I switched from using my foot to using my Achilles' tendon. I don't have to bend my right leg and it makes a nicer line for an audience.

I also keep my leg stationary and use just my left hand to throw the diabolo over my leg. Learning how to make the left hand pop the diabolo over the leg and then drop down to let it pass under the leg is much better than stepping down on the string. When you start trying different hop over points you will see why.

With the proper rhythm you can do a series of hop overs. Coordinate raising and lowering your left hand as the diabolo rolls near your foot so you don't have a collision. When the diabolo is back on the left side try another hop over.

Fig. 50. Hop Overs

Hop Over Thigh

Bring the string closer towards you and you can do hop overs using your thigh. The thigh acts just like your foot by cutting off the string until you lower your left hand to let the diabolo pass underneath (fig. 51).

Hop Over Waist

Another possibility is your waist or torso. Step over the string with both feet so the string is behind you and the diabolo is off to the left side. The left hand pops the diabolo up and over your waist to your right hand to make the catch as you lean over slightly backwards (fig. 52).

Fig. 51. Hop Over Thigh

Fig. 52. Hop Over Waist

Hop Over Both Hips

You can straddle the string and do hop overs around your hip. Once you get comfortable with each hip you can alternate between them (fig. 53).

Hop Over the Handstick

Here's a nice one. Grab a handstick length of string in your left hand. Now turn your left handstick so it is horizontal in the wall plane. Bring your right handstick over and in front of your left handstick. Now bring your right handstick back behind the wall plane and poke it through the loop of string hanging from your left handstick.

By pushing the right handstick against the string you can make the diabolo hop over the handstick (fig. 54).

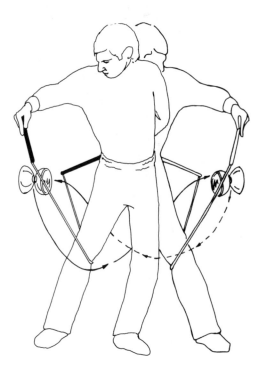

Fig. 53. Hop Over Both Hips

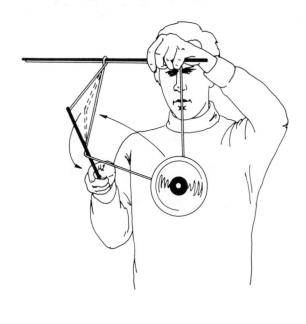

Fig. 54. Hop Over the Handstick

Hop Over the Arm

Hold your right arm straight out and bend your elbow up ninety degrees. Make sure the string is going underneath your right arm and the diabolo is between your right arm and the left handstick. Turn your right wrist back to keep the string in place. Now you are ready to do arm *Hop Overs*. Use your left hand to pop the diabolo up so it hops over your right arm, just above your bicep (fig. 55).

If you find that the string is too long to do this comfortably you can cheat a little bit. Grab a handstick length of string and run it along the left handstick.

Fig. 55. Hop Over the Arm

One Handed

There are two possible grips for the one handed diabolo technique. I prefer the first but try them both and see which one you like the best (fig. 56, 57).

Get a good spin going and transfer the handsticks into one of these grips. Now you keep the spin going with a lot of wrist and elbow rotation (fig. 58). Keep the diabolo level by moving the handsticks in front of or behind the wall plane.

Of course you will want to be proficient with both hands on this technique so you can try some other variations.

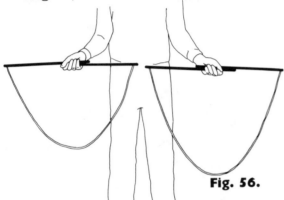

Fig. 56.

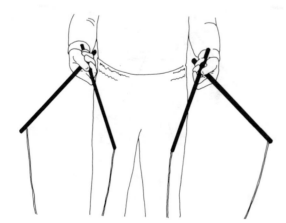

Fig. 57. Two Different Grips for One Handed Diabolos

Fig. 58. Pretend You Are Winding a Wrist Watch

Around the World Crossovers

Swing outside as in an Around the World and as you swing switch the handsticks from one hand to the other (fig. 59).

Two Fisted Diabolos

An impressive trick to other diabolists is to spin two diabolos at once, one in each hand (fig. 60). A warning, however, if you make it look too easy by practicing a lot everyone else will think nothing of it. Oh, well.

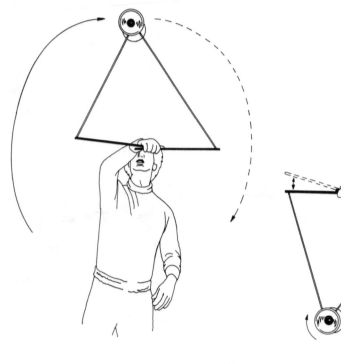

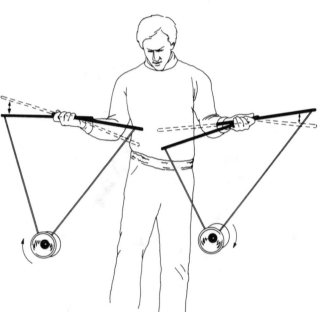

Fig. 59. Around the World Crossovers

Fig. 60. Two Fisted Diabolos

Other Tricks
Rock the Baby

Here's another yo-yo trick. Turn your handsticks in so they are both entirely within the wall plane.

With the diabolo coasting, place your left

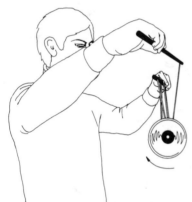

Fig. 61. Rock the Baby

handstick in front of and beneath your right handstick. Bring the left handstick in towards you making sure you pull in the string hanging from the right handstick with it. As you keep circling your left hand in and up, move your right hand forward and down. The right handstick now grabs two lengths of string as it circles in and up which is good because you want a nice, short length. End up with the left handstick directly below the right and you will have created a nice swing for your diabolo. See how nice the baby rocks? (fig. 61) .

Butterflies

It took me a while to feel comfortable with diabolos before I wanted to try this trick. There is something about barely-in-control objects flying near my head that says "caution".

Anyway, start swinging out to the left as if you were going around the world. When your hands are over your head and the diabolo is near the top of its orbit cock your wrists back so it descends behind you. On the next peak at the top cock your wrists forward and the diabolo will end up with no tangles back in home position. It helps me to imagine a figure eight type of pattern (fig. 62).

Fig. 62. Diabolo Makes a Small Circle Behind the Head

Loop Arounds

Have the diabolo coast a foot or so from the right handstick (fig. 63). Bring your right hand down and underneath the axle so the string no longer supports the diabolo (fig. 64).

Fig. 63. Loop Arounds

Fig. 64. Right Hand Circles Clockwise

Continue the movement up and to the outside, making one complete circle of the hand-stick around the free-flying diabolo (fig. 65). As you finish the circle again wrap the string around the axle (fig. 66). It helps to give just a bit of lift to the diabolo right before you make your circle to give yourself some more time.

You now have a half-loop of string around the axle. The diabolo still spins the same way but your left hand provides the power stroke. Reverse this move or switch your handsticks to get out of it.

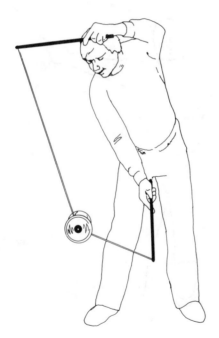

Fig. 65. And Comes Back Under Diabolo

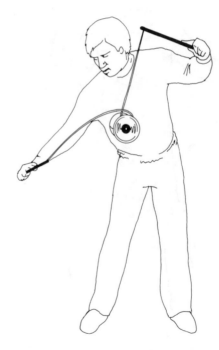

Fig. 66. Complete Loop of String Around Axle

Dynamic Pirouettes

Pirouettes were mentioned as a possible flourish while throwing and catching a diabolo. These pirouettes are done with the diabolo nearly always in contact with the string (when the trick is fully mastered).

I cheat a little bit and lift the diabolo up a foot or two so it is rising and falling while I am turning. This gives me a little extra time. The sequence for pirouettes is illustrated in figures 67, 68, 69, and 70. The real hot shots can keep the diabolo almost perfectly still while executing several pirouettes in a row, adding spin whenever the string is under the axle.

Fig. 67. Start

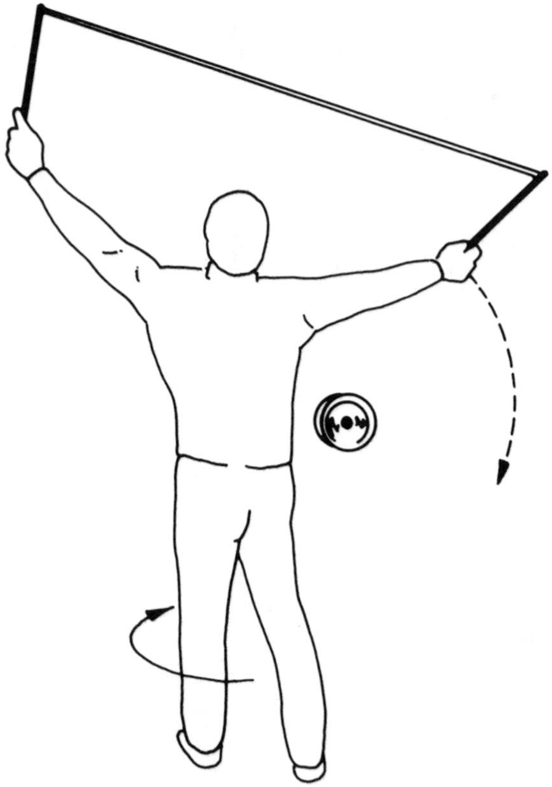

Fig. 68. Pirouette

To learn, have a friend hold a non-spinning diabolo in place so you can walk through these moves. He or she should hold the string taut underneath the axle of the diabolo while you do a pirouette. Notice how the string circles the axle and ends up back on the bottom?

That's it. Now all you have to do is to get your pirouette down fast enough so that the diabolo does not fall while you are turning.

Fig. 69. The Catch

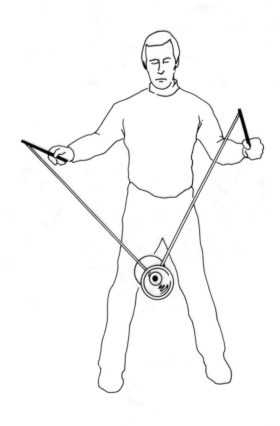

Fig. 70. Finish

One-Wheeled Diabolos

There is a type of diabolo that only has one wheel; the second wheel is replaced by a pointed tip (fig. 71). Once you get it going this diabolo can spin upright on its point like a top.

Since one end is inherently heavier than the other, the diabolo constantly tilts and changes its orientation, making you walk around in a circle. I personally don't use one-wheeled diabolos too much because I get dizzy.

Following are some tips for those of you who would like to try it.

Starting a one-wheeled diabolo is much harder than the regular kind. Put several twists on the string to give yourself time to get it up to speed and stable before you must start waltzing around (fig. 72).

Place the diabolo on the string with the point facing you and the wheel facing the audience. Turn the diabolo counterclockwise three times and start it off with a quick spin of your right hand as you let go. The diabolo will unwrap the twists while you are getting some speed. Once the twists are gone you must begin to walk around the circling diabolo.

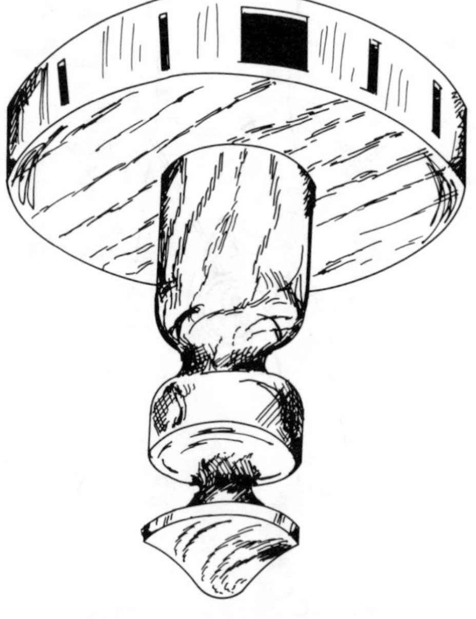

Fig. 71. One Wheeled Diabolos

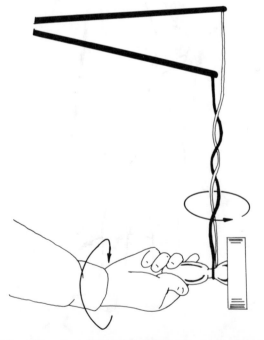

Fig. 72. Start with Several Twists in the String

In addition to all the regular diabolo moves you can also spin a one-wheeled diabolo on its point on the floor or in the palm of your hand (fig. 73).

Some variations of a one wheeled diabolo you might see are the Chinese performers using pot lids and ceramic urns (fig. 74).

Fig. 73. Diabolo Can Spin like a Top

Fig. 74. Master Xiuang Liang

Spinning Two Diabolos At Once

Now, I'm not just including this so you feel you must buy a second diabolo, it's a pretty impressive trick.

There are several ways to begin spinning two diabolos on one string. For the easiest method you need a partner. Have your partner stand to your left spinning the second diabolo. When you get your diabolo steady have him or her toss the second one over towards the string coming down from your right handstick (fig.75). The throw should not be high and you both need to be in the same wall plane with the diabolos aligned. I move forward and straddle across the wall plane to throw accurately.

The force of the second diabolo hitting the string descending from the right handstick helps the first diabolo fly from left to right in front of you. You also need to help it out with your left hand. You now have two diabolos doing a series of *Hop Overs* over each other. As each one rolls down the string spin is added to keep them stable.

Fig. 75. Partner Tossing In Second Diabolo

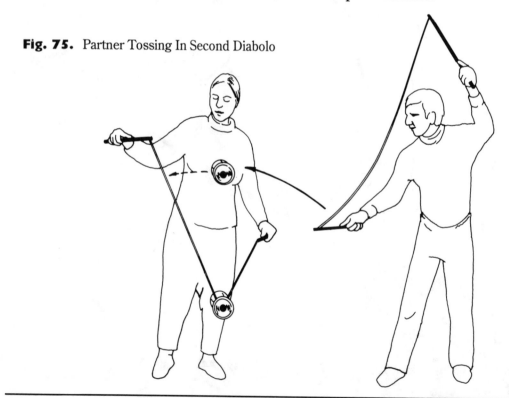

You can keep both diabolos spinning by lifting your left hand to do *Hop Overs*. You can even add spin by using your right hand. When each diabolo is heading down the string make a small whipping action down with the right hand to help it along. This adds quite a bit of spin to the diabolos (fig. 76).

Get one diabolo going and let it coast as you put both handsticks in your left hand. Grab a second diabolo and launch it with a low toss so you can catch it on the string to the right of the first diabolo (fig.77, 78).

The force of the launched diabolo coming down on the string causes the first diabolo to hop off the string over to the right. Since the second diabolo is not spinning too fast you should immediately add more spin by whipping your right hand down and to the left.

Fig. 76. Adding Spin with Two Diabolos

For the second method you should be able to launch your diabolo. By launch, I mean toss it from your hand with some spin so you can catch it on the string with control.

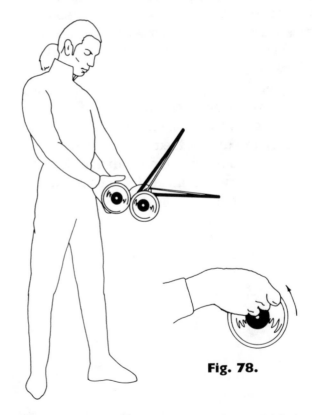

Fig. 78.

Fig. 77. Jochen Schell Set to Launch Two Diabolos

Correcting Tilts with Two Diabolos

Two diabolos may start tilting and turning in opposite directions. Using two different colored diabolos helps to see which one needs to be corrected.

The right handstick taps the misaligned diabolo just as it is about to land on the string on the right side (fig. 79). I tap on the wheel between the 12 to 3 o'clock position. Tapping the back wheel turns the diabolo counterclockwise as you look down from above, tapping the front wheel turns it clockwise.

This tapping technique may tilt the diabolos in opposite directions. If I change the wall plane slightly by putting my left hand in front of my right I can get them both to tilt in the same direction. Once I have both diabolos tilting the same way I can tap them back into proper alignment.

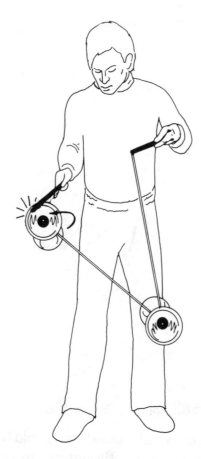

Fig. 79. Correcting Tilts with Two Diabolos

Variations with Two Diabolos

Here's Jochen Schell to show you some variations that you can do with two diabolos.

In the first trick with two diabolos, one diabolo is tossed up and spun on one handstick, while the other spins on the string (fig. 80).

Pop the diabolos up with the left hand and insert your leg into the pattern. Just watch the pattern for a while to get a sense of the timing and when to insert your leg (fig. 81).

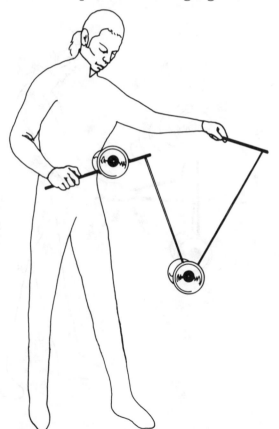

Fig. 80. Toss One up and Catch It on the Handstick

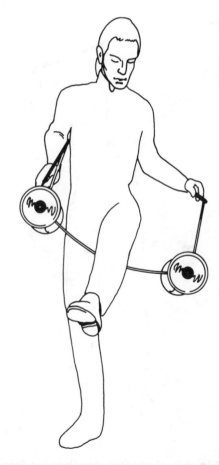

Fig. 81. Two Diabolos around the Leg

Use the same technique to get the diabolos to hop over your arm (fig. 82). I found it helpful to use two different colored diabolos for these two moves. After watching them go around and around I finally forced myself to go after the red one. Now !

Turn to the right and try an *Around the World* with both diabolos (fig. 83).

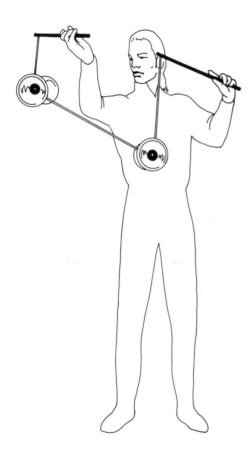

Fig. 82. Both Diabolos Over the Arm

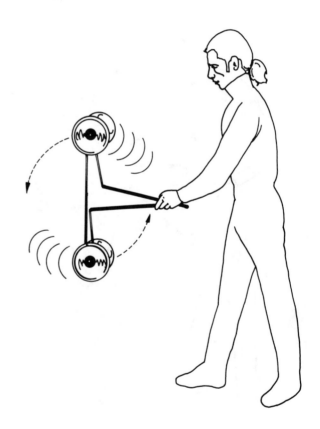

Fig. 83. Around the World
Each Diabolo Swings Over the Other

Throwing both diabolos high up in the air creates lots of new possibilities (fig. 84). Try a pirouette, or jump over the string.

If you can do a pirouette with two, why not try three? (fig. 85).

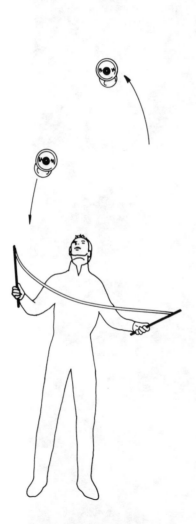

Fig. 84. Tossing Two Diabolos Up High

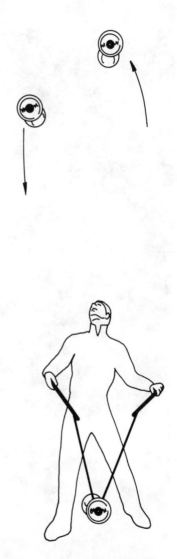

Fig. 85. Showering Three Diabolos

Gilles Le Leuch & Michael Korthaus

Photo - Verena Blank

3· Diabolo Play with a Partner

The most common type of partners work with the diabolo is to play catch. The chapter on advanced moves explains how to throw and catch a diabolo; we now only need to clarify how to throw to someone else.

De quoi parle-t-on à la ronde?—
Que l'on vante à tous les échos
Et qui fera le tour du monde?—
—LE DIABOLO —

Passing One Diabolo

If you want to throw the diabolo off to the side, keep your arm lower to the side where you are throwing. That is, if you throw to the right, drop your right arm. If you throw to the left, drop your left arm. As you open your arms to release the diabolo also fling them out to where you want it to go. Left for left, right for right (fig. 86).

You can also throw in front of or behind yourself (fig. 87). Just use your arms to direct the diabolo to where you want it to go. Here are some possible line-ups with your partner.

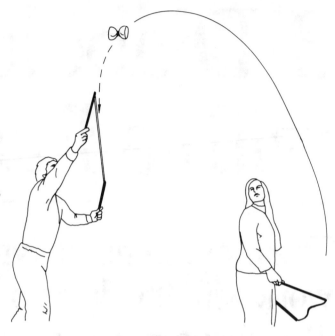

Fig. 87. Throw Behind Oneself

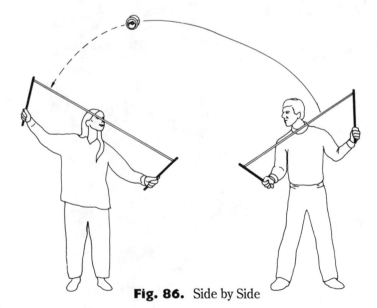

Fig. 86. Side by Side

For these two formations (fig. 88, 89),
one of the players must be able to spin with a
left hand drive.

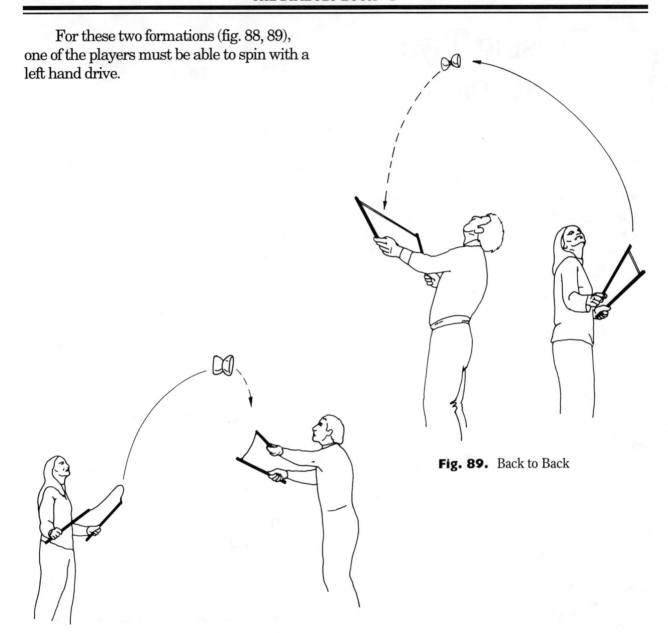

Fig. 89. Back to Back

Fig. 88. Front to Front

Passing Two Diabolos

Of course, if you and your partner like, you can try to work on passing two diabolos at once. The one on the left throws high and the one on the right throws low so the diabolos are caught next to the right handsticks to add spin (fig. 90).

Fig. 91. Three Diabolos

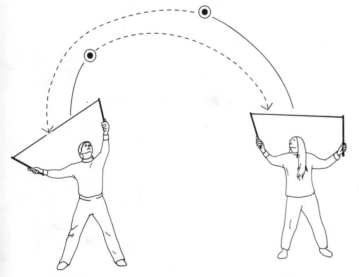

Fig. 90. Left Throws High, Right Throws Low

Juggling Three Diabolos

Extremely bold players may want to try to juggle three diabolos between them. A good pattern is the half-shower where the juggler on the right throws the diabolo inside and under the diabolo coming from the left. This way each player catches the diabolos on their right handsticks to add spin while the diabolos roll down the strings (fig. 91).

Steals

Instead of waiting for your partner to toss you the diabolo, why not take the initiative and steal it. Keep your string taut and come up underneath the axle to raise it up and off your partner's string. For this face to face steal one of you must use a left hand drive (fig. 92).

Steals from behind let both players use a right hand drive (fig. 93). Be careful so that the two sets of strings don't get tangled. Even easier, you can just grab the handsticks from your partner.

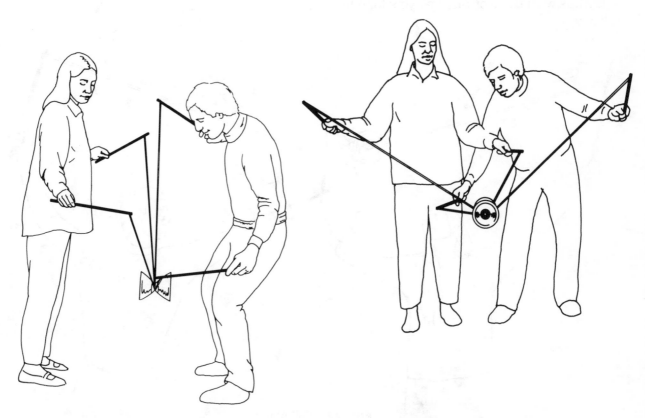

Fig. 92. Face to Face Steal

Fig. 93. Steal From Behind

Pass Alongs

Another nice way to pass the diabolo is to roll it from your taut overhead string onto your partner's string (fig. 94). If your partner can get the roll slow enough and you can get your feet fast enough, you can run around to the other side to pick up the diabolo from your partner again, continuous roll alongs. You might want to try this with three or more players for a line roll along.

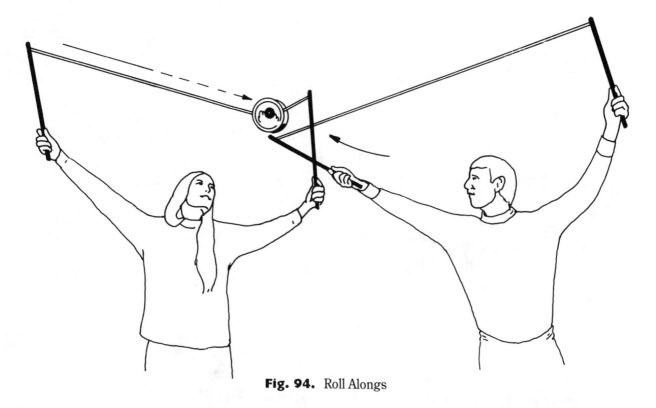

Fig. 94. Roll Alongs

Diabolo-Tennis

This was such a popular game in France at one time that people were afraid it would completely overshadow the current version of tennis.

Standard rules of tennis apply here with two exceptions: 1) players use only the back court, and 2) to serve you must line up facing one or the other of the side lines so the wheels of the diabolo are parallel with the sides of the court. You cannot throw the diabolo until you have a good, stable spin. If the diabolo wobbles or tilts in the air it is a loss of point to the thrower.

For those of historical bent, the official dimensions of the old French diabolo-tennis courts are 116 feet by 33 feet. Two lines 33 feet from the base lines are drawn to make two square 33 by 33 foot courts. You are not allowed to use the front court. The net is twice the height of a standard tennis net, or six feet. Parker Brothers, Inc. suggests 12 foot squares instead of 33 feet squares with an 8 feet high net in its instructions dated 1907.

To better cover the court you will want to be able to face either direction. It will therefore be a great advantage to be able to spin the diabolo with both a left and a right hand drive if one wants to excel at this sport. Diabolo-tennis, anyone?

The Diabolo Tennis Court Consisting of Two Trapeziums
From *Real Diabolo* by C. B. Fry, London 1907.

Various Postcards from
France and England,
circa 1908

4·History of the Diabolo

There are two questions that must be answered when discussing the history of the diabolo or any other toy: what is the origin, and how did it spread and become popular?

Origin

Like all basic toys, the exact origin of the diabolo has been lost. One would have as difficult a task trying to trace the origin of the yo-yo, the top or the ball. Most sources agree that the diabolo is a Chinese folk toy dating back hundreds or perhaps thousands of years. However, there is no clear path leading back to the very first diabolo. There is some speculation that it was also developed in Africa, for example.

Realizing the history is so imprecise I ask you to bear with me for a while. This chapter will attempt to cover the Chinese origins of the diabolo and its spread to Europe and North America. I will label my own inferences and opinions. Please forgive me if I spin off on a tangent now and again. If nothing else I hope my modest efforts will aid future research and researchers.

First Tangent, Into Africa

D. W. Gould, in his book *The Top*, mentions the possibility of the diabolo being played in Africa. He credits an illustration to Marcel Griaule showing a cylindrical object that looks a bit like a diabolo but would be very difficult to manipulate.[1] The French book *Le Diabolo Pour Tous* , also mentions explorers' accounts of central African tribes playing with a toy similar to a diabolo.[2] With the lack of collaborating support I doubt these claims. It seems as if the diabolo's exoticness is causing people to associate it with any place far away. For example, another source also states that diabolos came from both China and South America without giving any support for this position.[3]

Postcard, Algiers 1908

A Rose by Any Other Name

Mr. Gould uses an alternative name, *diavolo*, when describing the toy. This secondary name means "two sections in flight."[4] The term is used in other works though not widely. When first introduced in the West the diabolo also went under the name of *flying cones*.

In China the diabolo is called the *kouen gen, koen gen, kung-chung*, or *kong zhu*. The most frequent version mentioned in western sources is *kouen gen*. It apparently appeared during the Han Dynasty, 206 B.C.-A.D. 220.[5] Loosely translated this means "making the hollow bamboo whistle." The Pin Yin system of writing Chinese characters renders 'hollow bamboo' as *kong zhu*.

In ancient China the diabolo was originally called the *hollow bell*.[6] A Chinese friend says the characters, 空钟, actually mean "to make whistle or ring like church bells." Today it is referred to as the *hollow bamboo*, 空竹. Chinese diabolos are indeed hollow, made out of bamboo and whistle when spun. In the hands of a proficient diaboloist they are quite loud. Monsieur Bertin's book, *La Chine en Miniature*, published in 1812 has an illustration of a Chinese peddler using the sharp, whistling sounds of the diabolo to attract customers.

Although the written Mandarin characters are the same from province to province, Chinese has no formal, consistent oral translation into English. This accounts for the variations in spelling of the same characters. Notice the several different ways that the city of Beijing can be spelled. Or is it Peking? I am told by several Chinese scholars that *kouen gen*

Postcard, *Diabolo Skill* China

would be a transliteration from a very southern dialect of China.

The reason so many references use kouen gen, I assume, has more to do with later researchers relying on Monsieur Bertin's book and his original choice of spelling rather than the more popular Chinese usage. This is comparable to a foreigner visiting Boston and reporting back to his or her home country that the entire US population not only eats torpedo sandwiches rather than submarines, hoagies, or grinders, but does so with a New England accent.

Today the diabolo is played all over China during the Chinese New Year's Celebrations. In every street and lane you can hear the musical sounds of diabolos adding to the festivities.[7]

One can easily imagine how a simple toy as this was elevated into a performing art. Out of a natural talent or desire to excel some people became more proficient than the average player. For special holidays and festivals they were asked to show off a bit and demonstrate their facility with the diabolo. In this way the folk toy gained stature and became a performer's prop.

This elevation in stature has happened with other toys. Frisbee players hold tournaments where the better performers compete in different categories. Professional teams of Frisbee players travel the world putting on flying disc shows. In a similar fashion the United States had professional yo-yo and top spinners sponsored by Duncan not so many years ago.

You Can't Keep a Good Top Down

We are fortunate today to witness the revival of the diabolo and other circus and juggling acts in the People's Republic of China. On October 1, 1950, the first anniversary of the Chinese Liberation, Chairman Mao Tse-Tung and Premier Chou En-Lai witnessed a private performance of circus related arts in Peking. Out of this performance a national program supporting the circus arts and acrobatic troupes was begun.[8]

This program has proven to be quite successful. Circus troupes are not only sponsored by city, county, and provincial governments around the country, but the demand for this ancient style of entertainment is so great that some troupes are sponsored by the army, rural communes, and large industrial concerns. Today over eighty such troupes are active all over China.[9]

A standard set of circus acts is taken from the Chinese tradition of the *one hundred entertainments*. In this tradition some of the various diabolo moves have such colorful names as *fluttering butterfly*, *casting for fish*, and *crossing the bridge*.

Proliferation to the West

Though there are scattered references to the diabolo being enjoyed in Europe as early as 1470 AD, I could not find much support for this early date.[10] The strongest case can be made that the diabolo first began appearing in Europe in the 1790's. At that time the governments of Europe were very interested in developing increased trade with the Orient and other parts of the world. While European ships were allowed to land and trade in Shanghai, a southern port city, the interior of China was declared off limits to foreign traders by the emperor.

Lord George Earl Macartney was head of an English expedition in 1794 whose purpose was to try to set up an embassy in the interior of China for eventual improved trade relations with the entire country. The trip was considered unsuccessful. The party was allowed to stay only 67 days before being asked to leave by the emperor. However, the members were given views of everyday life of the Chinese that few other Europeans had seen.[11]

This interest in the Orient among Europeans is shown by the fact that not only did Lord Macartney publish his journal of the trip, but several other members of the expedition also published their diaries and journals.[12] The novelty and popularity of the Chinese spinning toy were so great, and Lord Macartney's failure to establish an embassy was so dismal, that social critics jokingly said the introduction of the diabolo to England was the most worthwhile result of the expedition. Referring to the diabolo, one person remarked, "And that was all the profit Europe had from the ambassadorship of Lord Macartney."[13]

A few years later some French missionaries stationed in China began sending back accounts and artifacts of Chinese life to a friend of theirs in the French government, Monsieur Bertin. In 1812 he had collected enough information to publish his book *La Chine en Miniature*, a guide for the French on the everyday life of the Chinese people.

I'd like to digress and introduce another Chinese folk toy at this time, the devil stick.

Postcard, France 1906-1908

The Chinese name is *hua kun,* which means 'flower stick.' It also uses two handsticks to manipulate a third hour-glass shaped object. The devil stick is much longer and thinner than a diabolo with no string attached to the handsticks. You bat a devil stick back and forth rather than spin it.

With the shared origin in names, the close approximation in shape, and the similar manner in which they are manipulated one can see that the devil stick and the diabolo are related. I like to think of them as first cousins. I'm sure the reason one encounters such few historical references to devil sticks compared to diabolos is because devil sticks are much harder to learn and never caught on with the general population.

A July 1823 poster advertising a German dinner theater performance by Indian jugglers Medua and Mooty Samme announces they will be performing not only the Chinese Stickplay but also with the Chinese Bells. The first item is a devil stick. By referring to the ancient Chinese bell term we can see that the name diabolo was not yet firmly fixed.

All these ambassadors, missionaries, and government workers visiting and writing about China were well-educated. Indeed, they had to have been in order to have held their positions of authority and responsibility. From the tone of the journals one also gets the impression that they were highly chauvinistic, believing themselves and their European culture to be much superior to the "heathen Chinese." One can eas-ily imagine their desire to bring back the artifacts of China, but the mood is of sharing oddities and novelties rather than serious cultural objects.

It's All Greek to Me

With this attitude there is no need to maintain the original Chinese names for these items. Instead they chose to apply their own names. Being educated people they spoke Greek, a mark of erudition. So, the toys were given new Greek names.

In Greek, the term *diaballo* means to throw across. It comes from a combination of *dia* meaning across or through (as in the *dia*-meter of a circle, a line that crosses a circle), and *bolla* or originally *ballo* which means to throw. We get the modern word *ballistic* from *ballista* which was a Greek weapon for throwing stones.

Postcard, France circa 1908

Speak of the Devil

Probably the two toys both went by several different names for a while, Chinese stick-play, Chinese yo-yo, Chinese bells, *diaballo*, *hua kun, kouen gen*, devil stick. In time *diabolo* was retained for the spinning version of the Chinese toy while the hitting version of the toy was rendered into English as the *devil stick*.

It is interesting to note that the term *devil* itself also is derived from the Greek word *diaballo*, meaning to throw across. A secondary meaning of diaballo in Greek is to slander or to traduce, to talk ill about somebody. If someone does not talk right at you but out of the side of his mouth about you, in essence, that person is slandering you. In political jargon today this slandering of an opponent is called *mudslinging*. Again, we have the connection between *diaballo* and throwing.

This slanderer (diabolos) shows up in the early Greek Bible. When Jesus Christ is fasting for forty days and forty nights in the desert, he is tempted by a diabolos. (Matt.4:1). From this general slanderer who is an evil spirit the term grew more specialized to mean The Evil Spirit, Satan, the one who can never talk straight. In Spanish we have *el diablo*, in French *le diable*, in Italian *il diavolo*, in German *der Teufel*, and in English *the devil*.

Postcard, France 1906-1908

From the original Chinese hollow bell, through the Greek language as the toss across toy, we now have in western culture the diabolo. Whatever you want to call it, it sure is fun.

The diabolo has also been called *the devil on two sticks*. Another way to think of this is the devil on stilts. The image of the devil on stilts is found in folk culture. A Welsh folk tale explains that Satan must wear wooden stilts as part of his winter disguise in order to pass among humans undetected. Without the stilts his cloven hoof prints would leave tracks in the snow, exposing his true identity. Borrowing on this idea Alain René Lesage wrote a French play, *Le Diable Boiteux*. In it the devil Asmadeus disguises himself as human and creates havoc in a village by letting all the neighbors in on each others' private family conversations.

Far from implying demonic possession we now know that the name *diabolo* is quite unrelated to any supernatural phenomenon. I have had many discussions with people out to save my soul from damnation but I still continue to play with this great toy. Of course, I live dangerously. I also eat deviled eggs and devil's food cake and have even ridden in a Cadillac Coupe de Ville. Anyway, now that the mystery of this devilish name is cleared up we can get on with the roundabout history of this fascinating toy.

French Revolutions

In 1816 the diabolo again shows up in the book *Le Juex de Quatre Saisons* as a popular children's pastime.[14] It was not only children who enjoyed the game but adults as well. The diabolo craze swept the upper classes of France around this time as a parlor game, with reports of some diabolos being made out of glass. The French also added a hook to the end of one of the handsticks that was used to catch the diabolo and perform additional tricks.

Illustrations around this time show well-to-do ladies and gentleman enjoying the

Postcard, France 1908

game. There is a sense of social satire at the expense of the upper class in these prints. One in particular shows several overweight gentlemen being spun into the air as if they, themselves, were giant diabolos. This probably reflects the close ties the diabolo shares with the yo-yo. Some years earlier the yo-yo was given the French name, *l'emigrette*. This derogatory term refers to the idle time spent by the upper classes that did nothing but play with the yo-yo and were ultimately forced to flee or emigrate to safety during the French Revolution.

Apparently players used the diabolo not just at risk of social criticism but of personal safety and property. French historian Henri d'Allemagne, notes, "The game of diabolo made its appearance in 1812. It soon became a passion, not only with children, but with grave gentleman and elegant ladies, who vied with one another in exhibiting their address, or lack thereof, to the great danger of costly mirrors and more or less valuable heads."[15]

In this same article Monsieur d'Allemagne also recounts the use of large diabolos being used in competition on the Champs Elysées in Paris. A rope 60 fathoms in length was supported in the middle by a pole 20 feet high. Two diabolos were sent up each side of the rope to see which would win the dispute at the top and drive the other down before it.[16]

In *The Top*, D. W. Gould mentions the existence of special diabolo clubs in Paris around this time with exotic names such as *Le Diabolo Club, Le Rochette, Le Devil Club* and *Club du Jeu de Diable*.[17]

Napoleon reportedly played with the toy. There is a print of the little corporal playing the game with his generals.[18] The 1927 Abel Gance film *Napoleon* which was restored and re-released a few years back has footage showing Eugène de Beauharnais, Josephine's son by a previous marriage, playing with the diabolo shortly before Napoleon and Josephine were married. Monsieur Gance did his homework. Napoleon and Josephine were married on March 9, 1796. A young boy of that time certainly would have diabolo. In an ironic twist a political cartoon of the period shows Wellington casually tossing up a diabolo with a concerned Napoleon sitting astride.[19]

Monsieur d'Allamagne also wrote several books on current and historic pastimes and recreations of the French. The diabolo is mentioned at some length in a few of his books as a popular pastime. A favorite graphic of mine is the color print, *La Manière De Jouer au Diable*, showing a devil with dozens of diabolos spilling out of his mouth. Along the borders are small hands demonstrating tricks with titles such as *le promenade, l'ascencion à corde tendue*, and *le Chevalet*.[20]

Resurgence at the Turn of the Century

The diabolo died out as a popular sport only to be revived shortly after the turn of this century. After seven years of research Gustave Philippart introduced a greatly improved version of the diabolo in 1906 with much better handling characteristics than the older style. He felt his new cone shaped diabolos not only made learning easier but allowed for more intricate tricks. In 1908 J. Hembert and P. Nivoix wrote the French book, *Le Diabolo Pour Tous*, that explains different variations and tricks. The authors felt the diabolo craze would continue longer this time because of Monsieur Philippart's new, improved design and the innovative use of partners' play with the toy.[21]

The game was indeed popular. On Thursday, May 23, 1907 a political cartoon by Albert Guillaume on page three of *Le Figaro*

Postcard, France 1908

shows two players with the fictional Ministry of Diabolo. The caption reads 'It's already not easy to make it fly, but it's even harder to keep it from falling.' (C'est déja pas commode de le faire sauter... mais c'est encore plus difficile de l'empêcher de tomber.) On May 28 of the same year the newly formed *Diabolo-Club* announced a large tournament to be held in Paris on June 9. Various tournaments were held around France that summer with players competing in different categories to see who could throw the highest and the longest as well as demonstrate the most originality with new tricks. A special treat at these exhibitions was the appearance of René and Marcel Philippart. I assume they are the sons of Gustave Philippart and had a virtuosity with the game that few others possessed. In December of 1907 *Le Figaro* ran ads for diabolos priced at French francs 2,95.

The following spring and summer of 1908 were also filled with diabolo demonstrations and competitions. On Wednesday, May 13 the *Kouen-Gen Club* sponsored a tournament for children at the Polo Fields. Competitions were held in spite of the rainy weather. The diabolo-tennis match was won that day by Monsieur Casteele.[22]

Yanks Spin Diabolos

An article published in the 1951 issue of *Jugglers' Bulletin Annual* says that in spite of repeated attempts to popularize diabolos they have only met with mild reception in the United States.[23] Parker Brothers sold a version of diabolo with instructions that are copyrighted 1907. The craze may not have been as big as in France but it was enough to make a teddy bear cry. A post card titled *The Fallen Idol* shows a tearful teddy bear holding a diabolo set with the caption, "And just to think-I had to take a back seat for 'diabolo'!"[24] I will leave it to other researchers to decide if Teddy Roosevelt once refused to shoot a diabolo. Collectors should note that quite a few post cards with diabolo themes were printed in various countries around this time.

Postcard, USA 1908

England Takes a Turn

Diabolos were, however, quite popular in England, though the indications are that it was not played with the same high skill level or competitiveness as in France. In 1908 David P. Ward published *Diabolo: the Game and Its Tricks* to bring the intricacies of the French style to England. Not only did he seek to expand the repertoire of tricks for the English, he was also interested in promoting the game of diabolo-tennis.

Mr. Ward was a bit late. The September 29, 1906 issue of *L'Illustration* already showed the techniques of the game with a photo of a London diabolo court. Their feeling was that it had a much brighter future than lawn tennis because it required not only more coordination and athletic ability but was more graceful.

The English took up the diabolo with a passion. Diabolo play was so popular that diabolos were used for political cartoons, were mentioned frequently in gossip columns, and were chosen as the subject for humorous articles and stories.

A.A. Milne, author of *Winnie the Pooh*, was an avid, if frustrated, diabolo player. He wrote not one but two different satirical stories for *Punch* titled *The Diaboloist*. In the November 13 issue of *Punch* a clever cartoon shows a pos-

sible solution to the railway dispute. Passengers using their own handstick sets are leaning out the windows of the train spinning all the diabolos attached to the wheels to propel themselves down the track.

Diabolos were also frequently mentioned in the gossip columns of the time. Several examples are scattered throughout this chapter. Interested readers should pick up some *Punch* magazines from 1907 to 1908 for others.

While I can appreciate Mr. Ward's zeal and enthusiasm, I am a bit suspicious of his claim that the diabolo is thousands of years old and is the precursor to the gyroscope used in modern torpedoes.[25]

Postcard, England 1914

Diabolos and Science

Though my pacifist nature wants to separate the gyroscopic diabolo from the torpedo it does pop up in scientific journals. C.V. Boys wrote several articles in the *Scientific American Supplement* demonstrating not only why shifting your hands forward and back horizontally will correct the tilt of a tipping diabolo but also explaining the ideal way it can be used in classrooms to demonstrate the physical properties of spinning and motion.[26] If you wonder why your diabolo does not always fly true Mr. Boys' explanation of how the spin affects flight will prove helpful. It has to do with the build up of air pressure due to the rotation.

Drawing on the work of Mr. Boys, Harold Crabtree also devotes some attention to the physics of diabolo in his book, *Spinning Tops and Gyroscopic Motion*.[27] Among other things the reader learns how to make a diabolo which will not spin.

What Goes Around Comes Around

I have run into quite a few people familiar with the toy from their childhood of fifty or sixty years ago. The English trade journal, *Games and Toys*, had several articles and advertisements in the thirties announcing the return of the popular game from the early 1900's. The same 1951 *Jugglers' Annual Bulletin* shows the dimensions for a diabolo that was made by Parker Brothers "some 12 or 15 years ago."[28]

More recently Parker Brothers again made and marketed a diabolo in 1967. Since then it seems to have fallen into relative obscurity, kept spinning by jugglers and handed down through their tradition of sharing skills and otherwise keeping each other frustrated with new tricks to learn.

Will the diabolo craze return in the nineties? One can always hope. Already jugglers are picking up the toy in ever higher numbers and coming up with new tricks and variations never seen before. Just as Monsieur Philippart's new design allowed for a higher skill level today's new diabolos are creating better and better players. Jochen Schell is astounding audiences with complex one, two and three diabolo tricks while the team of Michael Korthaus and Gilles Le Leuch is passing four diabolos. I suspect it will continue to have flurries of interest for quite some time.

Monsieur d'Allemagne was also aware of the changing nature of taste for this toy. In 1908 he wrote, "Unfortunately, the fickleness of popular taste in France will probably soon relegate it to oblivion, whence it may be rescued by some future antiquarian and made known to people for the third time."[29]

Mr. Boys also was aware of the fickleness of popular taste. Summing up his article on diabolos for the *Scientific American Supplement No. 1697* in July 1908 he said, "It may, and no doubt will, go out of fashion as quickly as it came in, if indeed it has not already done so, but that is not the fault of the game but of society."

Will the diabolo ever again become popular? I know I'll be spinning mine.

Mettons vite à profit notre science nouvelle
Et qu'un baiser d'amour sur la joue de ma belle
Prélude à nos joyeux ébats.

LE DIABOLO.

Postcard, France 1907

Postcard, France 1908

Notes

1. D.W. Gould, *The Top* (New York: Clarkson N. Potter, Inc. 1973) p. 178. Mr. Gould has included an excellent bibliography in his book. However, he incorrectly attributes the illustration in *The Top* to Griaule's book, *Jeux Dogons*. This illustration does not appear in *Jeux Dogons* but rather in Monsieur Griaule's book, *Jeux et Divertissements Abyssins* (Plate 1, #5). Although Griaule does label this toy a *diable* along with several other toys, his description indicates it is something other than a diabolo. It should be noted, for example, that Monsieur Griaule also calls a bullroarer a *diable*.

2. Hembert, J. and Nivoix, P., *Le Diabolo Pour Tous* (Paris: Duruy et Cie, 1908) p. 88.

3. Al G. Renner, *Experimental Fun with the Yo-Yo -and Other Science Projects* (New York: Donald, Mead and Co. 1979) p. 41.

4. *The Top* , p. 172.

5. Wen-Chung Wu, *Chung-hua t'i yü wen hua shih t'u hsüan chi* , (1975), p. 27.

6. Ch'u Pan She, *Chung-kuo tsa chi i shu*, trans. Zhan Gao, (Shanghai: Shanghai Wani, 1959) p. 62.

7. Ibid. p. 62.

8. *The Great Circus of China* , (performance program, Canada 1982).

9. Ibid.

10. *The Top*, page 172.

11. Lord George Earl Macartney, *An Embassy to China*, (Hamden, CN: Archon Books, 1963).

12. For a more thorough discussion of this European interest in China see Todd Strong's *The Devil Stick Book* (New York: Brian Dubé 1990) pp. 101-102.

13. *The Top* page 172.

14. Madame Deee *Les Jeux des Quatre Saisons, ou Les Amusements de Jeunage*, (Paris: La Librairie d'Éducation d'Alexis Eymery 1816), pp. 8-10.

15. Henri d'Allemagne, *Scientific American Supplement No. 1670* January 4, 1908, p. 12, translated from *La Nature* .

16. Ibid.

17. *The Top* p. 172.

18. Mrs. Nevill Jackson, *Toys of Other Days* (New York: Benjamin Blom, 1968) page 239.

19. *Banquet des Jouets & Jeux* (Paris: Marguery 1906) p. 22.

20. Henri d'Allemagne, *Sports et Jeux d'Adresse*, (Paris: Hachette and Co., 1903) pp.122-130.

21. J. Hembert and P. Nivoix, *Le Diabolo Pour Tous*, (Paris: Imprimerie Duruy & Co., 1908) page 89.

22. *Le Figaro*, Thursday, May 14, 1908, p. 7.

23. *Jugglers' Annual Bulletin*, (Tulsa, OK: Montandon Magic, 1952), pp. 47-63.

24. Susan Brown Nicholson, *Teddy Bears on Paper*, (Dallas: Taylor Publishing Company, 1985), p. 59.

25. David P. Ward, *Diabolo: The Game and Its "Tricks"* (London: Upcott Gill 1908) page 2.

26. C.V. Boys, "The Theory of Diabolo. A Scientific Explanation of a Toy's Vagaries", *Scientific American Supplement.t*, July 11, 1908, pp. 18-20.

27. Harold Crabtree, *Spinning Tops and gyroscopic Motion*, (London: Longmans, Green, and Co., 1909), pp. 39-41, 120-121.

28. *Jugglers' Annual Bulletin*, p. 49.

29. *Scientific American Supplement No. 1670*.

Afterword

You and the Diabolo

So, I hope this book has not only been helpful in showing you how to play with your diabolo but has also passed on some of the joy and magic of this marvelous toy.

Please don't think that all the possible tricks and variations are covered here. Instead, think of this as a solid beginning towards developing your art.

I am sure there are moves not mentioned in this book simply because I didn't know about them. There are also moves not covered here because they haven't been invented yet, that's your job.

Some people will continue to explore and play with the diabolo beyond this beginning level. Maybe you will not only invent new combinations of moves but also completely new moves. Please let me know about them. Some will go on to become professional entertainers with the diabolo and other juggling props. I'd like to catch your show.

You can use the diabolo as an entrance into the world of juggling. A natural progression is to learn other gyroscopic juggling forms such as tops, yo-yos, rope spinning, plate spinning, and Devil Sticks. Or you might take up toss juggling and other object manipulations.

There is a wonderful organization called the International Jugglers Association that I strongly recommend. They have a great magazine and host large and small conventions of jugglers in the United States. Contact the International Jugglers Association, PO Box 218, Montague, MA 01351. Tell them Todd sent you.

Many people may want to incorporate music and dance into their diabolo play. Others may want to work in groups doing large, synchronized routines. Whatever your leaning right now, enjoy the adventure.

I hope you enjoy this book and find it useful in learning how to play with your diabolo. Please do not think that this covers all aspects of the diabolo or all the possible tricks. There are as many tricks that are not covered here as there are imaginations to devise them.

Two obvious areas to explore are tops and

yo-yos. I have already given you some ideas and am sure there are more. Not quite as obvious is the world of juggling. There is a convention amongst jugglers to share their tricks so it should not be too difficult to get some pointers.

As you master the individual tricks also pay attention to your overall presentation. Which tricks seem to follow others well? Consideration should be paid to your posture and your delivery as well as your ability to perform the trick. Does it look nice? There is still much to explore and perfect within the field before going on to other areas.

Once you get the basic pattern internalized, look around and see what else is handy that might work as a diabolo. Try a yo-yo or a top. Over a well-padded carpet I am learning to spin brandy and wine glasses.

There Must Be Some Way to Use This in Swan Lake

The converse to using different props as a diabolo is to use the diabolo in a field other than what is covered here.

You might want to incorporate the diabolo into a dance. Some of the variations and moves would look very beautiful set to music.

In summation, this book is a start. If my modest effort is successful you will become intrigued enough to carry through on some of these ideas, or others you may come up with. There is still a world of possibilities to explore and nothing to stop you. Diabolos are inexpensive, portable, durable, harmless, and fascinating, a great hobby.

Even if you should master all the tricks in this book there are still new vistas. After ten years I have not exhausted all the avenues I would like to explore. Every time I pick up the diabolo there is something new, which keeps me a constant beginner.

Isn't that great?

Postcard, France circa 1908

Postcard, France circa 1908

Postcard, France circa 1908